Our Scars Help Tell Our Story

SCARRED

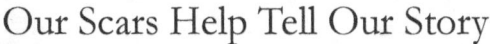

I0560569

Jacque Lacy

Not Just Alphabets Publishing
Las Vegas, Nevada

All Not Just Alphabets Publishing titles, AJ Houston, wordart, imprints and lines distributed are available at special quantity discounts for bulk purchases for sales promotion, fund raising, premiums, educational, institutional and library use.

Printed in the U. S. A.

ISBN: 979-8-9991547-2-9

SCARRED

Our Scars Help Tell Our Story

Jacque Lacy

Dedication

I remember my mother's words the day she received the first copies of her book, "Faithful Is He". It was the day after her birthday and an unexpected surprise. She repeated out loud and under her breath, I never thought I would see the day my book would be published. Heard her tell anyone who was willing to listen, how she worked on the content for twenty years because she did not want to forget or leave anything out. Put yourself in her place, imagine writing and not knowing if the words will ever see the light of day. We were always a family of love but the price of publishing believed to be slightly out of reach.

So this book is dedicated to time. Minutes, hours, years, days, to the vulnerability allowing you to share these moments of your life with strangers. It is dedicated to doubt, growth, faith, fortitude, the motivation to continue when self says stop. To every thought it took, every breath encumbered and deep, to sentences deleted and re written, to remembering and forgetting. Can't tell you how much courage is required to write the truth and be willing to tell your own story. Sometimes we will not be aware of our why. Why heaven chose you to go through these trials. Why family doesn't always family the way we think family should family. Why pain often is the companion of purpose, why purpose is not equipped with instructions or a how to manual. Why it is necessary to blindly pursue a task when the only familiar part is faith. This book is dedicated to faith, to love, to the blood of Jesus, to the Scriptures memorized. To all the Bible verses mom taught us, to the drills of who could find the book of the Bible the fastest. You won't know what drives you. It will take everything you've been through, every heartache, every trial, every course conquered, every battle won, every loss you turned into lessons. Every hug, every kiss, every child, every grandchild, every niece, every nephew, brother, sister, aunt, uncle, grand on both sides. It will take everything and everybody just for you to find the best you. And I must say this is the best you big sis. The very best you. It is an honor to help you tell your story.

-aj houston-

Table of Content

From Scarred

Introduction 8

When I Was Very Young 10

It Was A Rough Recovery... 12

As A Teen and Young Adult 24

As An Adult... 30

My Scars, My Flaws, My Secret............ 34

our scars help tell our story

What I Learned 56

Reflections 81

Acknowledgments 82

About The Author 83

Contact Information 84

Introduction

Have you ever seen a young person sitting in a corner in a room full of people? Have you been in class, group activities, meetings or part of a team and no one heard what you had to say, because you actually said nothing? That was me! I was extremely shy, once I got burned. I felt damaged, inferior, like I no longer mattered or had value because I had gone through severe trauma which left me scarred!! I was a young girl still forming my identity, at least in my own mind. Recently, I was speaking to a friend who was doing an assessment on me and she asked me a question that had to do with thinking back to the most devastating memory that had impacted me.

For me, it was the burn I suffered from hot cooking oil. It spread over my small arm and leg while trying to prepare my item for the class party that day, at the young age of nine. While thinking back, reflecting and recounting this incident to my friend I inadvertently admitted that the scar I received could have just as well been plastered across my face by the way I acted, wore it, saw it. I covered it up so that no one else could see it. She was floored by that admission because she had known me forever, even during that time frame and yet she never knew the impact of that incident and all the lasting ramifications that revolved around it. I became very good at hiding my feelings of inadequacy and imperfection... or at least I thought I was good at it, sometimes even to the extreme. I remember the song, "Still Water Runs Deep" and until I got older, I really did not understand what that meant. It is very true I realized later, as I was a very deep and analytical thinker however, I rarely shared my thoughts with anyone.

So, for this reason I was attracted and drawn to the person sitting alone, or the quietest person in the group or on the team, I knew they had a lot to offer, just as much as anyone else - once they felt safe enough to open up. All that was me, which is why I am writing this Book.

I like many others needed to be set free. I tried everything I could think of to get past my issues but until I began to truly see myself as God sees me, I remained stuck or at the least vacillated back and forth. Scripture says, in John 8:36, "Who the Son sets free is free indeed!" I have been set free. Through your faith and trust in the finished work of Christ, my prayer is that you too can be set free from the scars of life. Those that are visible and those that are invisible. Also set free from the havoc our scars can heap on the way we do life. We just have to believe with our whole being... mind, body and spirit, then we can release the bondage and walk in freedom!!!

It Happened
When I Was Very Young

When I was a young girl, nine years of age, in the fourth grade I was supposed to bring popcorn to school for a party we were having. I went in to fix the popcorn by first heating up the cooking oil in a skillet on the stove. When the oil, or grease as we called it back then, was extremely hot I was getting ready to pour in the popcorn kernels, but dropped the bag onto the floor. As I bent down to pick it up the bottom of my dress brushed the skillet handle and it came tumbling down and fell on the floor but not before the oil drenched me while I was leaning down. It was caught and held primarily in the left sleeve of my dress as well as in the tights I was wearing to school that day. This changed me forever! I was Scarred for Life!! Everywhere I went the scar was with me. Again, it could have just as well been going across my face for how prominent it was to me.

It Was A Rough Recovery...

This was the hardest thing to date that I had ever experienced. It was extremely painful. My brother Ray was standing near me, I think he was also cooking something, so after the skillet fell and the oil splashed on top of me I obviously went into shock, or so I was told. I began screaming so loud and so repetitively, "Ray did it! Ray did it!! Ray did it!!!"

I simply could not grasp what was going on or what had just happened to me. I was screaming but I was unaware it was as if I was I was outside of my body witnessing an incident that I could not fully understand. The only way I could make any sense of the event was to blame it on the closest person to me. Our mother ran in and saw what was happening and she immediately and instinctively grabbed at my clothing and pulled the dress along with the sleeve away from my body in order to stop the burning pain, and all of the skin came off my left arm right along with it! The same thing with the tights I was wearing

our scars help tell our story

It turned out that I had suffered 1st, 2nd, and 3rd Degree burns on my left arm and leg.

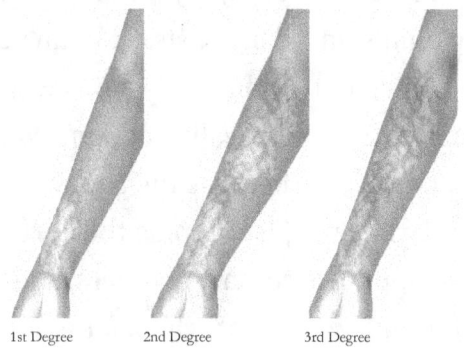

1st Degree   2nd Degree   3rd Degree

Along with the removal of layers of my skin once the garments were grabbed and abruptly snatched off, the burn was so deep that even my nerves were exposed. The pain from something like this is indescribable. When my mother actually took me to Baylor Hospital in Dallas, we found out that pulling the clothes off the way it was done probably caused even more damage.

I know my mother just did what most people would have done because the main objective at the time was to remove the problem at it's source. I was traumatized. I had a long journey ahead of me, one that I felt I was on alone most of the time. My burns would ooze and run then they would dry up and stick to the bandages. It was a long tedious, painful and odious process to soak and remove the large nonstick pads and gauze. I remember I would cry and cry and cry. Eventually my mother taught me to take care of the cleaning and changing and dressing for my burns. I had to learn to soak, remove, clean, apply ointment, change and redress the wounds on a daily basis. I couldn't go to school, I had to stay home, first because infections were always a possibility and successfully healing at home was of the utmost importance. Also because the pain was unbearable and it was a full time job just keeping the burns clean, dry, and away from the close contact of others, it was all consuming. I think I was out of school for at least three (3) months, maybe more just trying to heal. All the while experiencing excruciating pain along with what I now believe was anxiety and depression.

Reflections

Reflections

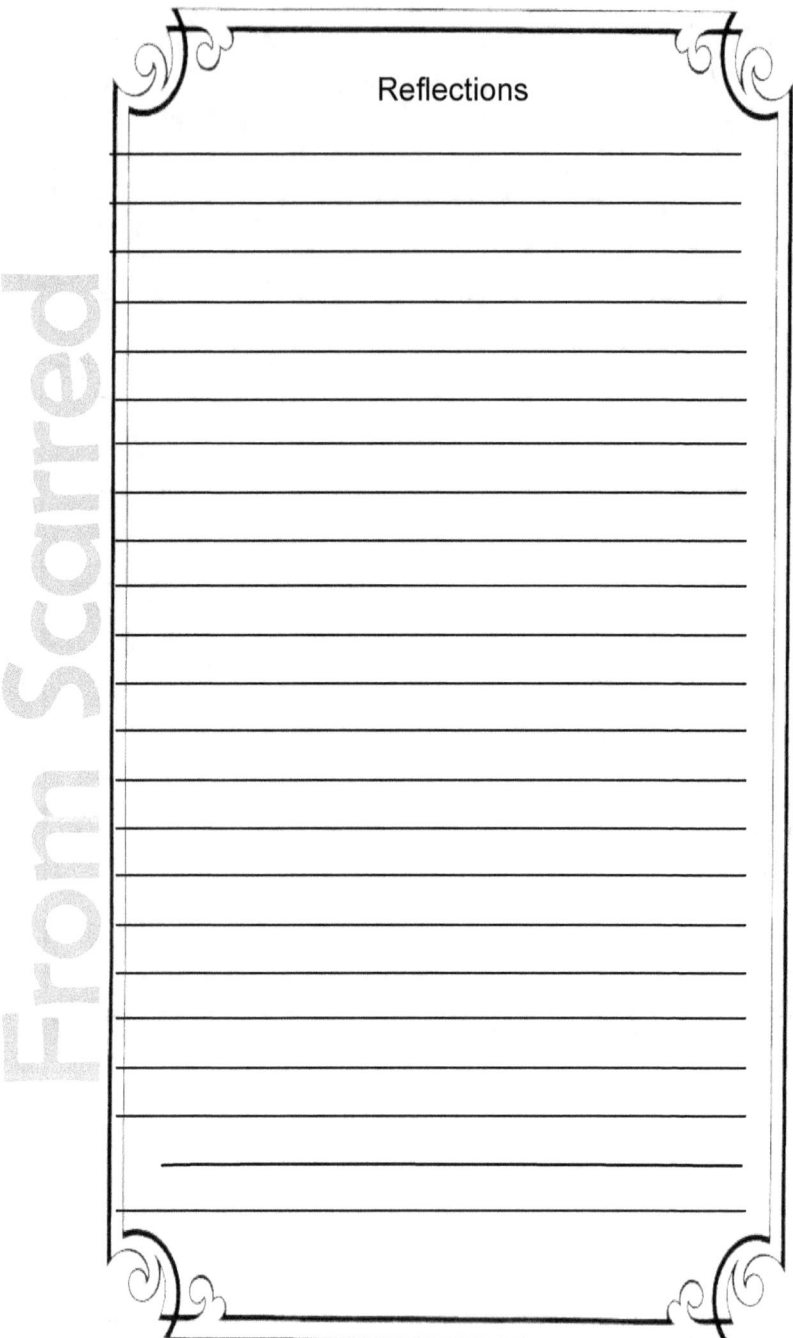

our scars help tell our story

Reflections

To Perfection

Additional Trauma Of Being Teased In School...

When I did get to go back to school, I was very nervous and scared. I felt like an Alien. I felt different. I felt out of place. I felt damaged. I felt flawed! Even though my arm was still wrapped up in bandages I felt naked, like everyone was looking at me and they could plainly see my imperfections, they could see that I was flawed, this too was scarring.

To prove my point, one of my male classmates would call out loudly whenever he would see me, "Burnt Arm!" He would repeat it over and over at every opportunity. Then he would put his head down on his desk as if he was innocent and hadn't done a thing. It really hurt my feelings and made me cry inside and out. My brother would come to check on me often just to see how I was doing. He had made himself my protector staying close between classes so that no one would inadvertently bump into me. When I told him about the things my classmate was doing he threatened to beat him up and the teasing stopped. However, the sting and shame from the teasing remained with me because I still knew what he and maybe even others were thinking. I went inward and became a shell of who I previously thought I was because I felt inferior to others who I saw at that time as perfectly whole. It's amazing how traumatizing things can be to a young person and so hard to shake.

our scars help tell our story

Reflections

Reflections

our scars help tell our story

Reflections

To Perfection

As A Teen and Young Adult

I was limited in my clothes choices. I never wore anything that did not have long sleeves. I also didn't wear shorts. I dressed very modest. Not because I was a Christian, or a God fearing young lady, and I was, but because I was hiding. The teen years are really significant in helping to shape your future choices in life. It is a time of transition from childhood to adolescence. I took this same mentality into both phases. It was a normal thing for me to not let people know I had been burned and scarred. I just kept that part of my life and history hidden, my own little secret. It was hard enough to be accepted by your peers when you really are not being accepting of yourself.

I remember not wanting to go to the swimming pool with my siblings because I had to wear a cover-up the entire time. I learned to wear a T-shirt over my swimsuit to camouflage and hide. I would always wear extra-large (XL) T-shirts even though my correct size should have been small (S) or extra small (XS). I did this so my arm and leg would be covered. That practice remained until just recently... no one understood why I would always get an XL

T-shirt no matter what the event, that way I had a large collection to choose from. At that time church groups, school groups, work groups, and other groups and organizations would provide or sell T-shirts for various outings or activities so everyone participating could be identified at a glance. Some groups still do. I was an avid collector of extra-large T-shirts and wore them exclusively to ensure adequate scar coverage, for me this was a necessity.

our scars help tell our story

Reflections

Reflections

From Scarred

our scars help tell our story

Reflections

As An Adult

This bleed over into Adulthood. I was so used to hiding that it was just what I did. I was presenting and perpetrating as if I was flawless when I knew I was not. Somehow through camouflage and fashion, I thought I could make everyone else believe I was.

When I met my now and forever husband at the place where we both worked, I was pretty shy. I had come out of a less than successful marriage that took place shortly after I graduated from high school. I originally married my longtime boyfriend whom I'd met the summer after completing the 8th grade. I was fourteen (14) years old when we first met. Ironically, he was a lifeguard at our local swimming pool and our Church chose this park and pool to have a Church Family gathering.

This new man that showed a lot of interest in me at my new place of employment did not know my secret. I was a pro at hiding. My first husband and I were separated for a extended period of time and eventually divorced. Then with all the attention I was receiving from so many eligible bachelors, along with the increase in money I was making, it just made me cover up even better. It seemed I had it all together, it seemed I was very confident, and as long as I was covering my scars... I was!

Reflections

our scars help tell our story

Reflections

My Scars, My Flaws, My Secret

I saw the scars as my flaws and something no one needed to know about. However, when my now husband, then boyfriend from work, and I got closer with each other, I knew at some point he would have to know. Eventually, I finally sheepishly and shyly revealed my scars to him and he unflinchingly, looked, lightly stroked, and then kissed my scars. According to him, they didn't make a difference or change anything about me. I knew he was special and that God had prepared him for me and me for him.

our scars help tell our story

It was the exact opposite with my first husband. He would constantly feed my insecurities and point out every flaw he could find. He would say things like, "Look at all those scars on your legs." "Where did all those scars come from?" He also would say to me when I thought I was dressed up and was getting ready to go somewhere, "Where are you going with all that clown make-up on?" He even told me at one point, in no uncertain terms, that no one would want me but him, I may have felt similarly as well, because of the many scars on my body. He had accepted me, but would anyone else? This man, as unsympathetic as he was, was my first child's father. Being as small as I was, about 100-105 pounds, having my beautiful daughter left me with an episiotomy scar and stretchmarks. Scars, scars, everywhere, although those associated with childbirth did not haunt me as much as the burn scars did, probably because they were covered up anyway.

Joe, my second and forever husband was nothing like the first. He just loved me, scars, flaws and all. He supported me, and encouraged me in all my variety and ever changing endeavors, I changed directions plenty of times. Together we created a handsome son and Joe has been a wonderful husband, father, provider, lover of me totally, and my soulmate. He even adopted my daughter and made her his very own.

He came into her life when she was about three (3) years of age and we were married by the time she was six (6) years old. They have always been 'thick as thieves', as the saying goes, and they would always side with each other when my husband and I would disagree about something. Our son came along when our daughter was seven (7) years old and he was the completion of our little family unit. While our daughter took my husband's side our son would side with you on a more situational basis. He would choose sides based on some criteria, that only he knew what it was. You never really knew what side he was going to take, so we always had to make our best argument or defense, but it was usually all in fun!

Reflections

our scars help tell our story

Reflections

To Perfection

Do I Really Believe God or Do I Just Talk Like I Do

I have made many decisions in life that did not serve me well, but meeting and marrying Joe and having my beautiful children are definitely not on that list. We know and understand when God is in the midst of things, they can change drastically, and for the better. That is definitely what happened in my case and I believe the result can be the same for anyone who seeks Him with their whole heart. He loves us and longs to hear from us, to help us, to heal us!

I finally began to realize that I did not always believe about God what God believed about me. As it is written in His Word in the first Chapter of Genesis, especially in verses twenty-six through twenty-eight (Genesis 1:26-28). We have a royal inheritance that we don't fully realize or accept. God made us in His own image and wants us to reflect His Glory in the world. He continues to find ways to show us Himself in order to convince us of what He already thinks and knows about us. However, it seems that we are so eager to exchange the truth for a lie; then we start hiding. It was true all the way back to Adam and Eve in the Garden of Eden. Things were perfect and when their curiosity got the best of them and they fell for the lies of the enemy. Things went totally awry, perfection ceased to exist for humanity and what did they do, they tried to hide. Even though they were unsuccessful, because no one can hide from God! This is a clear example that hiding is a useless waste of time and the truth will eventually come to the light.

Reflections

From Scarred

our scars help tell our story

Reflections

I had wasted so much of my time and everyone else's not focusing on what is most important in life... such as being satisfied with who God made me; productively using all the gifts and talents He gave me; being a good example of godly living for my family and others; grateful for His forgiveness, grace and mercy; walking in the Authority and Anointing He gave me as a Minister of The Gospel; and believing all He said about me in His Word.

I was only hurting myself because no one else really cared about the superficial scars I bore and hid. However, I had placed so much importance on external scarring and I felt that even if no one saw the scars they somehow made me less than perfect. I was not fully acknowledging that I am less than perfect because I am an imperfect human being, in need of a Savior just like everyone else.

Unfortunately, I had allowed the scars on my body to penetrate deeply through to my mind and my heart and affect every aspect of my life. It was time to forgive myself and move on, for God had already forgiven me for any shortcomings or any disbelief, or any and everything else because I had already put my trust in Him at a young age. I heard someone on a Talk Show mention what their definition of forgiveness was, and I really liked it, it was something like, "Forgiveness is giving up the hope that the past will ever be different!" The quote is not verbatim but the gist is that we can't change our past but we can certainly react differently to it once we realize it can never be changed. Unfortunately, it takes some of us longer than we would have liked it to take to actually accept this truth.

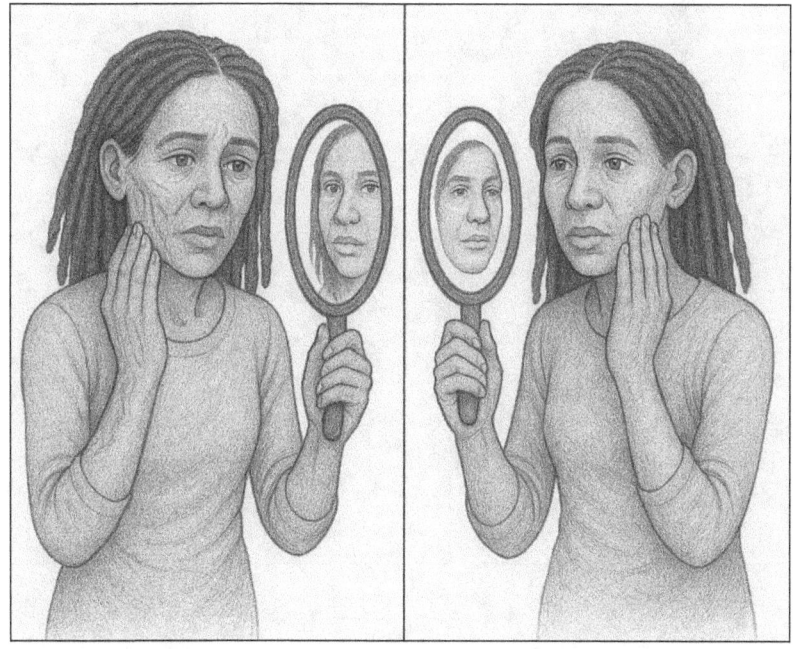

Before   After

Perception is not Reality

We must realize the greatness and purpose inside of us, and when we do, we won't have the luxury of being less than our best.

our scars help tell our story

our scars help tell our story

Reflections

From Scarred

our scars help tell our story

Reflections

Maybe you have some scars that no one knows about. Maybe you have been hiding for a very long time because it just got easier not to have to deal with the pain associated with the scars... how you got them, what impact they had on your life, who knew and who didn't; what could be done about them; what couldn't be done about them... so many variables, who wants to deal with all that stuff???

God does... even when we think no one knows or no one sees or cares His Word reminds us in Psalm 55:22, "Cast your cares on the LORD and he will sustain you; he will never let the righteous be shaken."

I remember venting to my sister at one point, telling her all the things my husband had said, what he had done, and why I was sooo angry at him. I can't even remember what I was complaining about, I just remember my sister's response (after I had just ran down all the offenses of my husband), "Is that all? Is that what you are so mad about?" "Girl," she said, "That's not even a real problem. If that is all you have to worry about you are doing good!" And she laughed! It was a stark reminder that many things are relative and based on personal experience. What is catastrophic for some may not affect someone else the same. God made us that way as well. We are all individuals with different and unique experiences and this uniqueness can inform the way we react or choose not to react to certain circumstances.

I don't presume that my scars are deeper or more devastating than anyone else's... I am here to highlight the fact that scars, despite their level of severity, have a profound impact on the lives of the scarred.

There are so many things that leave scars. Some scars are completely invisible but significant none the less. There are also so many people that play a part in the shaping of who we become, including parents; siblings; relatives; teachers; preachers; friends; enemies; classmates; coworkers; this is not an exhaustive list however, no one should have more say or influence than the individual themselves and God. We have been given the Authority to be and say what God has said about us.

Even though in some cases there are things we have done to cause our scars and even though there were some things that were done to us without our consent, when we were powerless to change our situation (and sometimes we simply felt we were powerless) as in child abuse; sexual abuse and molestation; domestic violence; sex trafficking; prostitution; witnessing or being the victim of violent or criminal behavior; serving in the armed forces... and so many other things have scarred us for life but we don't have to hide the scars nor the pain. We are not the things that happened to us!!!

1st Peter 5:7 (AMP) tells us that we should be, **"casting all your cares [all your anxieties, all your worries, and all your concerns, once and for all] on Him, for He cares about you [with deepest affection, and watches over you very carefully]."**

At one point, I remember lying in the bed and as I glanced in the mirror on my side of the room, I could barely see the scar on my arm. I kept looking closer and harder, it was practically indistinguishable from the skin surrounding it. I realized I had been so used to seeing myself as scarred so that even when they were diminished, I was unable to tell or even notice. It left me wondering how long the scars were fading or were not as prominent and I just ignored it. This let me know that the scarring that took place was as much in my mind as it was on my body. I was actually seeing something that clearly didn't even look the same.

Reflections

Reflections

From Scarred

our scars help tell our story

Reflections

What I Learned
About Scars From Jesus

Jesus was not afraid to display His scars. He wore them proudly because of what they meant to the world. His scars remind us of what He went through, not because He did anything wrong, not because He deserved the terrible treatment that was responsible for the scars, not because they changed who He was at any point, inside or outside. He was still perfect... He was God Incarnate!

So tell me why I being human felt all my life that my scars changed who I am, like they made me less than others, damaged goods. It's like I had to be ashamed that I had been hurt and scarred as a child through no fault of my own. When its really put into perspective, God's perspective, I realize I am still made in the perfect image of God. He made me just like I am and it did not surprise Him in the least that this scarring would take place. Thinking back to that day, I am grateful that not only did I survive the 1st, 2nd, and 3rd Degree burns as my skin succumbed to the hot oil that soaked my clothing that school morning,

our scars help tell our story

scalding and scarring me for life. I realize God sparred me from having my face included as the hot oil splashed on the left side of my body as I kneeled down to pick up the popcorn I had dropped. I cannot imagine how I would have managed if the burns would have been on other parts of my body, my face in particular, since I was so obsessed with the scar on my arm and leg.

I am so thankful that I have become aware that God never saw me the way I saw myself. He has always seen me as beautiful. It was me all along thinking of myself as less than… but not anymore. I choose to see myself as God sees me! If Jesus, being God saw His scars as something to be celebrated, then who am I to see my scars as something to be hidden and a source of shame? This shift in focus has led me to better understand that I am an Overcomer, I am a Survivor, I came through a tragic and traumatic situation that could have yielded a much different and devastating outcome… But God!!! God in His infinite wisdom and by His grace and mercy, rescued me. Now instead of being shameful I am grateful.

I would love to say that I just came to myself and realized this, but It came straight from The Word of God and if I say I am a Believer, I must start with what God says about me, allowing His definition to supersede my own. He is the final Authority! He created me to bring Himself glory and to assist in stewarding the Kingdom of God. All the while helping to bring the chaos of this world under the Authority of Christ by the power of The Holy Spirit which is at work on the inside of all God's children of which I am happy to be counted among.

If you are among the Scarred, we can change our thinking and our behavior by acknowledging who we are based on the following 10 Amendments, which by no means is a complete list… just enough to get us on the right track.

our scars help tell our story

Remember what God says...

THE TEN AMENDMENTS

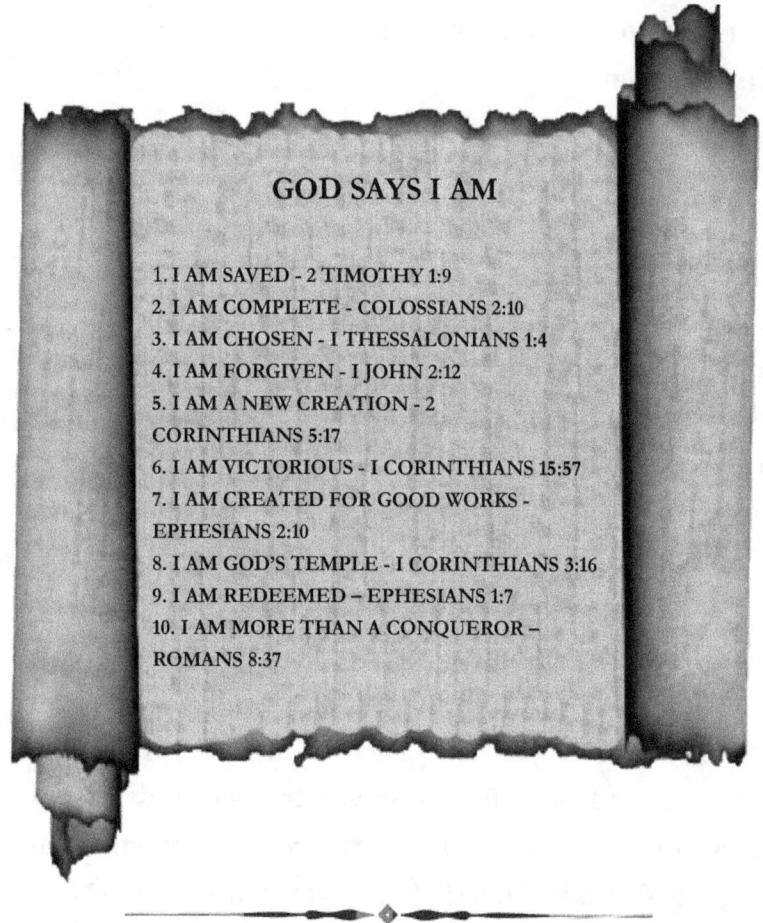

GOD SAYS I AM

1. I AM SAVED - 2 TIMOTHY 1:9
2. I AM COMPLETE - COLOSSIANS 2:10
3. I AM CHOSEN - I THESSALONIANS 1:4
4. I AM FORGIVEN - I JOHN 2:12
5. I AM A NEW CREATION - 2 CORINTHIANS 5:17
6. I AM VICTORIOUS - I CORINTHIANS 15:57
7. I AM CREATED FOR GOOD WORKS - EPHESIANS 2:10
8. I AM GOD'S TEMPLE - I CORINTHIANS 3:16
9. I AM REDEEMED – EPHESIANS 1:7
10. I AM MORE THAN A CONQUEROR – ROMANS 8:37

From this point on I will not be ashamed of who I am...the good, the bad, or what may appear ugly to some, because my scars are a great reminder of the fact that I came through a tragic event. Even though I allowed them to hold me back in many ways, not any longer. I will recognize how much work and sacrifice has been done on my behalf by my Lord and Savior. I received this promise according to Deuteronomy 31:8, which says, " **The LORD himself goes before you and will be with you; he will never leave you nor forsake you. Do not be afraid; do not be discouraged.** "

We are not the things that happened to us. Again, we are Overcomers. We just have to act like it! Sometimes we take up residence when all we should be doing is referencing. I heard a Doctor say something similar while speaking on a totally different subject, but it struck me as applicable, because I was living scarred. When I should have been using my scars as a point of reference for particular occurrences in life that I had successfully come through. Not becoming entrenched and stuck, daily living in the past.

John 16:33 tells us how we should be walking in peace instead of hiding out of fear that others will see the real us, concerned about what they might think if they truly saw us... scars and all..."**I have told you these things, so that in me you may have peace. In this world you will have trouble. But take heart! I have overcome the world.**"

our scars help tell our story

Additionally, the song, *"What A Friend We Have In Jesus"* reminds us of the peace we often forfeit and the needless, unnecessary pain we bear just based on feelings not facts, not taking everything we deal with to The Lord God in Prayer. He has the Power to change our trajectory no matter what path we started on.

Scars for most of us are inevitable and just like our Savior, we can wear them as a badge of honor (something we made it through) or we can hide them and try keeping them under a bushel, or doing whatever we think will work, so no one can really get to see us or get to know who we really are. Jesus shows both His scarred hands and the scar in His side, when anyone really wanted to know if it was Him. It's always better when we are real and not hiding who we are out of fear of rejection or because of perceived flaws. We are happier when we can be transparent with those we know and love!

I can tell you with certainty, hiding is draining and it takes on a life of its own. It limits the choices we make when God has provided a multitude of opportunities for us. I do not want anyone to take the path I had chosen for far too long. Hiding so that no one could see what I saw as imperfection, only makes us unable to be all that God wants us to be. He wants us to be free.

Scripture reminds us in John 8:36, **"He who the Son sets free is Free Indeed!"** I learned that it takes more than just reading, more than just a head knowledge of something, even more than just a heart knowledge... it has to get down into your feet. We must walk out what we know! We can't just keep thinking about what we need to do, we can't just keep talking about what we need to do, we need to actually be about doing it. Especially when we see it spelled out in The Word of God like we see in.

Philippians 4:6-9:

"Do not be anxious about anything, but in every situation, by prayer and petition, with thanksgiving, present your requests to God. [7] And the peace of God, which transcends all understanding, will guard your hearts and your minds in Christ Jesus.

[8] Finally, brothers and sisters, whatever is true, whatever is noble, whatever is right, whatever is pure, whatever is lovely, whatever is admirable - if anything is excellent or praiseworthy - think about such things. [9] Whatever you have learned or received or heard from me, or seen in me - put it into practice. And the God of peace will be with you."

our scars help tell our story

Though scars may come and scars may go, some may even be permanent...but because they are a part of life, may we never allow our scars to keep us in turmoil and strife. May we allow them to teach us and grow us...not misguide and throw us!

If we could just follow the example that Jesus set... He could have gotten rid of His scars if He wanted to and none of us would be the wiser, however, He chose to keep them forever.

He used them as a reminder of how much He loves us.

I remember asking God to remove my scars because I knew He could, I remember buying every product imaginable to try and clear up the scars, I even remember going to doctors to see what they could do. They only made things worse. I had a skin graft done in my thirties or forties and the doctor discussed the procedure with me prior to surgery. I thought that I would wake up from the operation with less of a scar not more. The surgeon made a decision while I was under anesthesia to change the donor site (the area they would remove the skin to place over the burn scar). Instead of removing the skin from the backside as planned he chose to take the skin from my thigh. It left a worse scar and created a whole new area of scarring. I did not know beforehand that I had the type of skin that was prone to scarring…I was one of the millions with keloid skin. So, now I not only had the two burn scars on my arm and leg I also had the donor site scar on my thigh to worry about.

Imagine being a young, skinny, stylish, fashionista that had three huge scars to hide everyday at all times. It was a lot of extra work. Just for a visual, the scar on my left arm measured approximately six inches long and three and one half inches wide (6"x 3.5") and it covered the upper area of my arm down past my elbow with additional less serious splatter scars up to my shoulder; the one on my left leg was about three inches long and another three inches wide (3"x3") it was shaped similar to a butterfly (at least that is what I was told); the donor site scar was also six inches by three and one half inches (6"x 3.5") located on my upper thigh, it turned out to be the worst of all of the scars. It's as if trying to work things out on my own backfired.

 I finally began to understand that God being Sovereign wanted me to learn something from my scars. It makes me think of what Jesus' scars meant to the Disciple's when they saw Him after He had completed His work on the Cross. To really recognize and know that He was who He said He was His scars were used to definitively identify Him. His scars were unique to Him and were a precious reminder that

Jesus had given up His life, albeit temporarily, to ensure we could have life eternally. He did all this just so when we believe in Him we can have a place with Him in Heaven for all eternity. We know some doubted, but hopefully we don't follow that model. May we follow in the way of true Believers, not like the Disciple dubbed *"Doubting Thomas".* **"the disciples were together again, and this time Thomas was with them. The doors were locked; but suddenly, as before, Jesus was standing among them. "Peace be with you," he said. Then he said to Thomas, "Put your finger here, and look at my hands. Put your hand into the wound in my side. Don't be faithless any longer. Believe!"** *(John 20:26-27)*

*Some of us need to see to believe
and some of us believe simply because we trust God!*

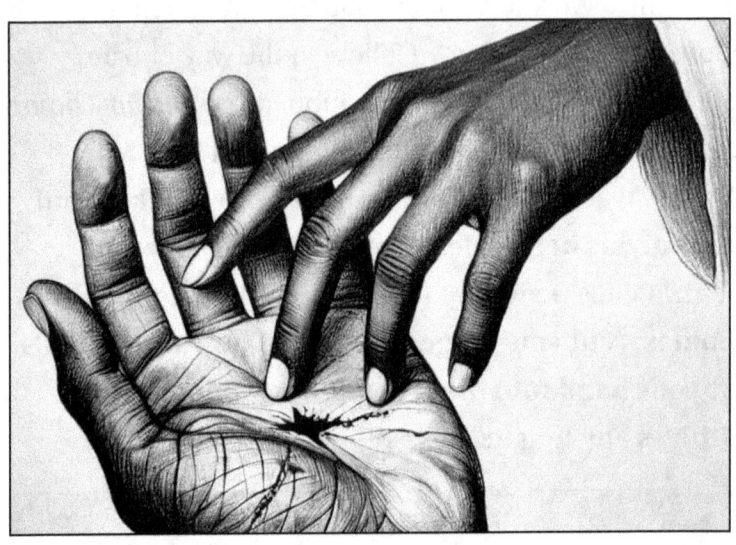

It really doesn't matter if you are not able to identify with my scars or the way they have affected me, because we are all so unique and different. You may have come through something a lot more difficult or devastating. There are so many things that leave severe scarring on our minds, bodies, and souls. Some scars have been even left on our hearts. However, all scars have meaning and purpose and help to facilitate the plan God has for our lives. He never wastes a circumstance... each one (in the long run) is for our good.

Some of us require a blueprint to help us manage our lives, and The Word of God certainly gives us everything we need to live in this world successfully. However, I am also keenly aware that many of us are accustomed to and need a type of *12 Steps Program* like Alcoholics Anonymous has, which has been a life saver to people too numerous to count and it is well thought out and has proven very effective in giving its participants a new chance at a more productive fulfilled life.

For our purpose, in order to condense this information and process I have attempted to put together a *Step Program* that I believe can help us condense and synthesize a lot of this information and help us change our way of thinking which in turn changes our behavior. Since it is said that *Seven (7)* is the number of perfection, and because God created the Heaven and the Earth in *seven(7) days*, I decided to add my *Seven (7) Steps* for successfully scar proofing our minds, at least they have been very helpful to me. I hope this is something that you too can benefit from.

7 Pillars for Successful Scar-Proofing Your Mind

1.   Select a trusted like-minded friend to confide in... it's always better to have at least one other person you feel comfortable talking to where both parties can be completely honest.

2.   Serve others in some capacity on a regular basis... there are so many opportunities for service to others who are hurting, in need, scarred in some way, and are less fortunate than ourselves.

3.   Seek God's Kingdom Agenda more than our own agenda... His has eternal implications while ours is fleeting and temporary.

4.   Share something we are thankful for every day... write it down, profess it audibly or tell someone.

5.   Start taking less serious things less seriously... life is too short to worry about things we are unable to change or control.

6.   Speak love and life not gloom and doom... our words have power we have what we speak.

7.   See ourselves as God sees us... He made us, He knows us, He chose us, He loves us... unconditionally.

our scars help tell our story

God has gone so far as to give us new names to assist us with accepting our new identity. He calls us:

- Righteousness [of God] (2nd Corinthians 5:21)
- New Creation (2nd Corinthians 5:17)
- His Workmanship / A Masterpiece (Ephesians 2:10)
- Redeemed (Ephesians 1:7)
- Forgiven (Ephesians 1:7)
- Child of God [Adopted not an orphan](Ephesians 1:5)
- Holy and Blameless (Ephesians 1:4)
- Blessed (Ephesians 1:3)
- Chosen (Ephesians 1:4)
- Royal (1st Peter 2:9)
- Special (1st Peter 2:9)
- Victorious (1st Corinthians 15:57)
- Salt of the Earth (Matthew 5:13)
- Light of the World (Matthew 5:14)

Think about the importance of Jesus' scars and how humanity could be saved because of them. Not forgetting that based on the decision we make to believe or not to believe in Him has real life and death implications of eternal consequence and impact, and it just makes my scars seem so insignificant. I would 'venture to guess' that your scars will appear less significant when compared with the impact of the scars of our Savior. I declare and decree that I will no longer be concentrated and fixed on such things as past personal scars... even though they used to plague and consume me, because now I can see that they really don't matter anymore. Actually they never really did, at least not to the degree that I fixated on them.

My eyes and my concentration must continually shift to The Cross and the Work Christ Jesus did because He knew we were not able... left to our own devices. He did this not because of anything we have done, but because of all God has done to make sure we are covered, secure, beautiful, and whole. We are complete in Him with His perfect plans, promises and awesome opportunities created for us before the foundation of the world. All we have to do is put our trust in Him believing He is who He says He is and that He can do all He says He can do!

our scars help tell our story

WE ARE CREATED IN GOD'S IMAGE – GENESIS 1:27 GNT

So God created human beings, making them to be like himself. He created them male and female,

WE ARE UNIQUELY AND WONDERFULLY MADE – PSALM 139:14 NLT

Thank You for making me so wonderfully complex! Your workmanship is marvelous---how well I know it.

GOD HAS A PLAN FOR OUR LIVES... AND IT'S MUCH BETTER THAN OURS - JEREMIAH 29:11-12 NCB

For I know full well the plans I have for you, plans for your welfare and not for your misfortune, plans that will offer you a future filled with hope.

GOD DIDN'T JUST WAIT FOR US TO CHOOSE HIM… HE CHOSE US FIRST – EPHESIANS 1:4-5 CEB

God chose us in Christ to be holy and blameless in God's presence before the creation of the world. God destined us to be His adopted children through Jesus Christ because of His love. This was according to His goodwill and plan.

our scars help tell our story

Reflections

Reflections

our scars help tell our story

Reflections

Now, in my sixties, I am wondering why in the world did I wait so long to be and show up just as I am.

I feel like I wasted so much time that could have been used to really make a difference in the lives of other scarred individuals. We have all been through something, some of us more than others! As I live and breathe (since so many people I've known can no longer say that), I am becoming more fulfilled and thankful and even more focused on legacy... what kind of example have I been to my children and family; also Kingdom Building... what am I doing that lifts up the Name of Jesus Christ and how pleased would He be with my actions. Now, I do not want to squander or lose out on anything God has promised or set aside for me due to any insecurity or fear on my part. After all, isn't it He that promised to surely allow 'His Goodness and His Mercy to follow me all the days of my life!' *(Psalm 23:6a)* And one thing we know for sure is that **"He who promised is Faithful!"** *(Hebrews 10:23b)*

I Prayed and asked God to give me something profound, something impactful, something that might leave an imprint on someone facing issues with scars, whatever they might be or however they present themselves or impact one's life... I heard Him speak to my spirit, ***"Your Scars Help Tell Your Story!"*** The response came so quickly that I could do nothing but laugh. ***"My scars help tell my story,"*** I repeated. Then I laughed again as I asked, ***"Lord is that You?"*** I wondered silently, (as if He would not know what I was thinking) ***"Is that the best we can do?"*** I kept hearing the same thing so I went with it.

What I want you to remember is what God told me, **"YOUR SCARS HELP TELL YOUR STORY!"** Your real story!!!

You don't have to wait to tell your story or let people know who you really are. Please do not wait as long as I did. We have been fearfully and wonderfully made in the Image of Almighty God. He knows all that we have gone through, He knows everything we have done as a result and He loves us unconditionally. Sometimes it's hard to comprehend that kind of love... but the fact is, we have it anyway. God has promised to never leave nor forsake us and He means it. We can take Him at His Word!

If you, like me, have been shrinking back because you wanted to keep your scars hidden and covered up, that is no longer necessary. We can reveal and uncover our scars because they are there to help us tell our story...The Real Story... the one that brought us to the point where hiding is no longer an option. It is never too early or never too late to be all that God intended for us to be!!!

In JESUS' NAME AMEN

Reflections

From Scarred

our scars help tell our story

Reflections

Reflections

our scars help tell our story

Reflections:

We all have come a long way from where we started. Which in turn defines each and every one of us as Overcomers. It was not my intention in the beginning to tell this story. God gives each of a message and a mission. What you hear and how you accomplish yours is up to you. This book unbeknownst to me became mine. And here I am, sharing my life with you. I hope my truth helps you in some way, and I pray now you are able to share your truth with whomever you deem it necessary. I guarantee they will be blessed in the telling. We are all endowed and blessed with Purpose, as you seek to find yours tell the world and help someone discover their Purpose too.

The sections labeled Reflections are strategically placed here just in the slightest instance you discover something about you relative to the topic. Please feel free to add your thoughts. Write down what has impacted you and let it be the beginning of working through your story, from scarred to perfection. Thank you for purchasing this book.

Tag, you're it. Now go and tell Your Story.

With A Sincere Heart - Jacque

Acknowledgments

First and foremost, I give honor and glory to God, whose grace, wisdom, and strength carried me through every step of this journey. Without Him, this book - and the lessons within it would not exist. To my beloved mother, Birdie Lee, thank you for your godly teaching and for living as a shining example of faith and integrity. To my father, Jimmie Jay, your steadfast and unwavering commitment and love have been a constant anchor in my life. To my husband, Joe, the love of my life, my staunchest supporter, and the very definition of "soul mate," your belief in me has been unshakable. You have walked beside me in every season, and for that, I am forever grateful. To my children, Carla and Jorell, and your wonderful spouses Terrance and Ashley, I love you deeply and continue to learn from you every day. You inspire me to grow, to listen, and to lead with love. And to my amazing grandchildren, Terren, Kyler, Keelon, and Caidyn, you are my heart and my legacy. You have given my life renewed meaning and purpose, showing me a kind of love I never knew was possible. My special dedication to you: May you learn from the mistakes of our generation, walk boldly in wisdom, and never repeat them. To my family, my siblings, and my Publisher, Thank You for encouraging me even when I felt like giving up. To everyone who played a role in my journey, whether in big ways or small, please know that I see you, I appreciate you and I love you. This book is a testament not only to my story, but to the power of faith, perseverance, and the unbreakable bonds of family. May it inspire those who read it to walk in love, live with purpose, and leave behind a legacy worth remembering.

our scars help tell our story

About The Author

Jacquelyn Jaye Houston Lacy is a retired telecommunications professional, ordained minister, and dedicated community leader whose life's work reflects a commitment to service, mentorship, and faith. With over 25 years in the telecommunications industry, she advanced from entry-level assembly to mid-management, earning numerous outstanding service awards, all-expense-paid trips, and performance bonuses along the way. Following her corporate career, Jacquelyn served as a church secretary before stepping into full-time ministry as a Mentor Coordinator. In this role, she connected at-risk students, starting in 4th grade - with caring mentors, guiding them through high school graduation and beyond. Her passion for shaping young lives is rooted in her belief in what God says about each individual, and she continues to invest her time and energy into the next generation.

A graduate of Wilmer Hutchins High School, where she was Homecoming Queen, Miss Senior, and ranked 7th in her class, Jacquelyn went on to earn a dual BAS degree in Business and Communications from Dallas Baptist University, graduating Magna Cum Laude. She has been an ordained and licensed minister of the Gospel since 2012 and proudly holds two Distinguished Toastmasters (DTM) Awards, the highest honor in Toastmasters International. Today, Jacquelyn remains deeply active in her community. She mentors and encourages students at DeSoto High School, serves as secretary for the DeSoto Police Clergy and Community Organization (DPCC), and volunteers as a Citizen on Patrol (COP) with the DeSoto Police Department, acting as the department's eyes and ears in the community. Beyond her professional and volunteer work, Jacquelyn treasures her role as wife, mother, and grandmother. Married to her loving and supportive husband for over 44 years, she is the proud mother of two exceptional children and grandmother to four "awesome" grandchildren. Her legacy is defined not only by her professional accomplishments, but also by her unwavering faith, servant leadership, and dedication to uplifting others.

Contact Information

Email scarredjjl2025@gmail.com

FB   facebook.com/jacque.lacy

IG   instagram.com/jaye.lacy